Copyright © 2025 by Daoudi Publishing LLC

All rights reserved. No part of this publication may be reproduced, distributed, or transmitted in any form or by any means, including photocopying, recording, or other electronic or mechanical methods, without the prior written permission of the publisher, except in the case of brief quotations used in reviews or scholarly works.

This journal is intended for personal use and reflection. It is not a substitute for professional mental health care or counseling. If you are struggling with grief or emotional distress, please seek help from a licensed counselor or healthcare provider.

Published by Daoudi Publishing LLC
ISBN: 978-1-960809-19-3

# Dad I Keep Searching for Answers...

A Guided Grief Journal
for Coping with the Loss of a Father,
Healing, and Expressing
What Is Hard to Say

**Evelyn Harrington**

I Keep Searching for Answers Journals

# TABLE OF CONTENTS

Introduction ............................................................................................. 1

How to Use This Journal ...................................................................... 2

## BUILDING A SAFE PLACE TO BEGIN

Dealing with the Shock of Loss Statement ................................... 9-10

Accepting the Truth Little by Little ............................................... 11-12

## NAVIGATING COMPLEX EMOTIONS

Sorting Through Confusing Thoughts ........................................... 15-16

Facing Fear and Moving Forward .................................................. 17-18

Handling Anger in a Healthy Way ................................................. 19-20

Letting Go of Regret and "What-Ifs" ............................................. 21-22

Free Yourself from Shame ................................................................ 23-24

Breaking the Silence .......................................................................... 25-26

## THE TURNING POINT

Coping with Feeling Alone ............................................................... 29-30

Managing Deep Sadness ................................................................... 31-32

Holding the Memories ...................................................................... 33-34

## FINDING MEANING AND RELIEF

Finding Small Moments of Peace ................................................... 37-38

Making Room for Acceptance ......................................................... 39-40

Honoring the Past with Gratitude .................................................. 41-42

Keeping Father's Love in Your Heart ............................................. 43-44

## EMBRACING HOPE AND GROWTH

Finding Hope Even on Hard Days ................................................. 47-48

Healing and Strength ........................................................................ 49-50

Self-Care While You Heal ................................................................. 51-52

You Are Not Alone on This Journey (A Gentle Message for Bereaved People) ................................................................................................. 53-54

The End ................................................................................................ 58

# INTRODUCTION

*By Evelyn Harrington*

Grief is not just about loss, it's about learning to live with love that has nowhere to go. If you are holding this journal, know that whatever you're feeling is valid. The pain, the questions, the memories, and even the silence, all of it deserves space.

Losing a father changes everything. You may find yourself searching for answers, replaying moments, or wishing for words left unspoken. You may feel overwhelmed or unsure of what to feel at all. That's okay. Grief isn't a straight path, and healing isn't about forgetting, it's about making room for what you carry inside.

This journal is here to support you, offering a safe space to express, reflect, and process at your own pace. The prompts inside will help you navigate loss, honor your emotions, and remind you that you are not alone.

Write when you're ready. Be honest with yourself. Your story, your grief, and your love for your father will always matter.

With warmth and understanding,
*Evelyn Harrington*

# HOW TO USE THIS JOURNAL

*There is no right or wrong way to use this journal. Some prompts may feel natural to answer, while others may be difficult. That's okay. If a prompt feels too heavy, you can:*

- Write without stopping for one minute. Don't worry about grammar, structure, or making sense. Just let your thoughts pour onto the page, unfiltered.

- Pause and take a deep breath. Give yourself permission to feel without judgment.

- Write from someone else's perspective. Imagine what your father might say to you, or how a friend would respond to your emotions.

- Read the prompt out loud. Saying the words first can help you process them before writing anything down.

IF YOU EVER FEEL STUCK, START WITH:

- Write down what you can answer today. If a prompt feels too big, break it down. Answer just a small piece, and leave the rest for another time. Some prompts may feel easier with time.

*This journal is here for you, without expectations or timelines. Use it at your own pace, in whatever way helps you process your loss. Every word, every pause, and every tear matters.*

This Journal Belongs To:

*Amanda leigh*

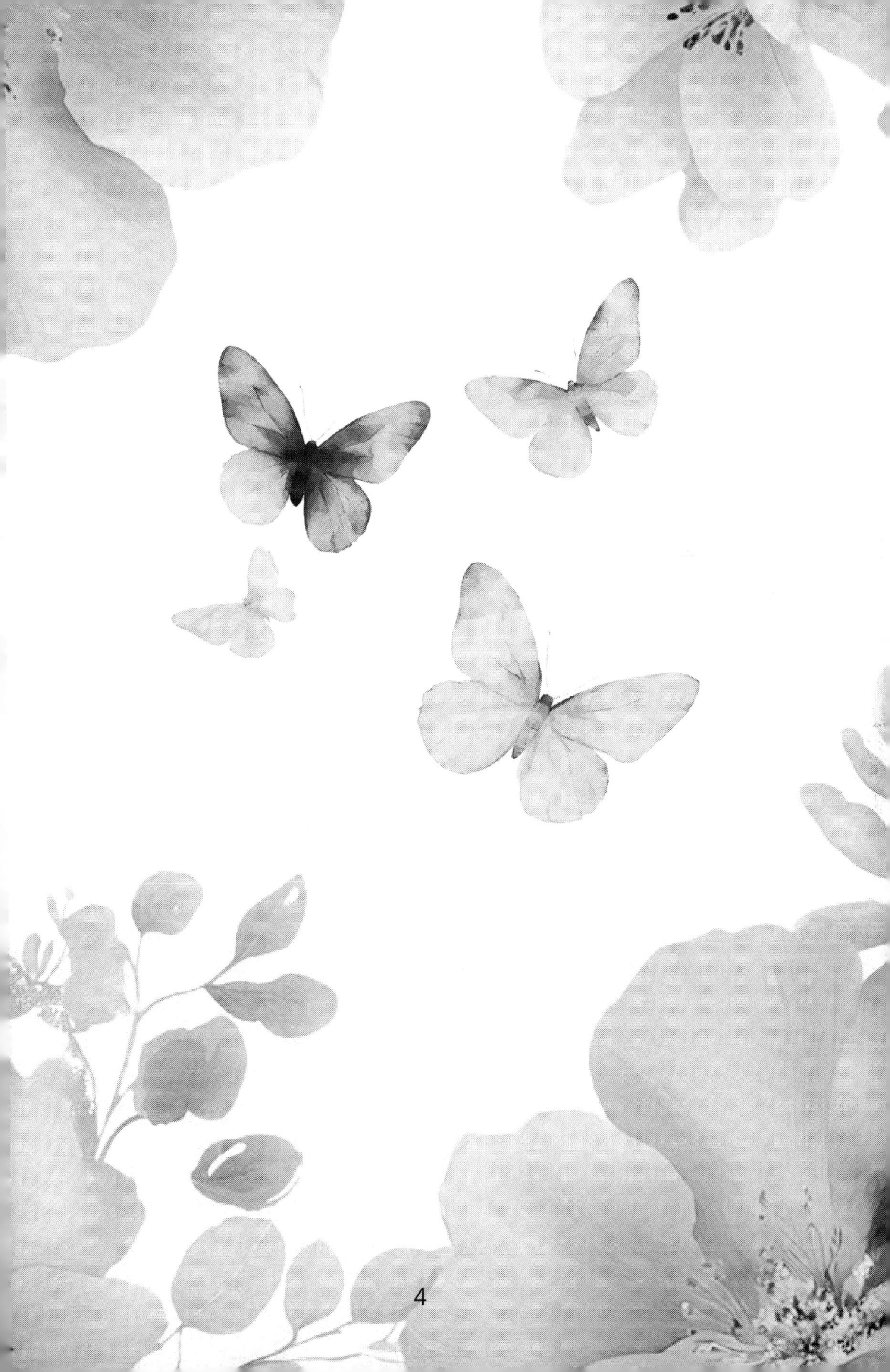

# MY FAMILY TREE

"Family is like a tree, its roots keep us grounded, and its branches help us grow."

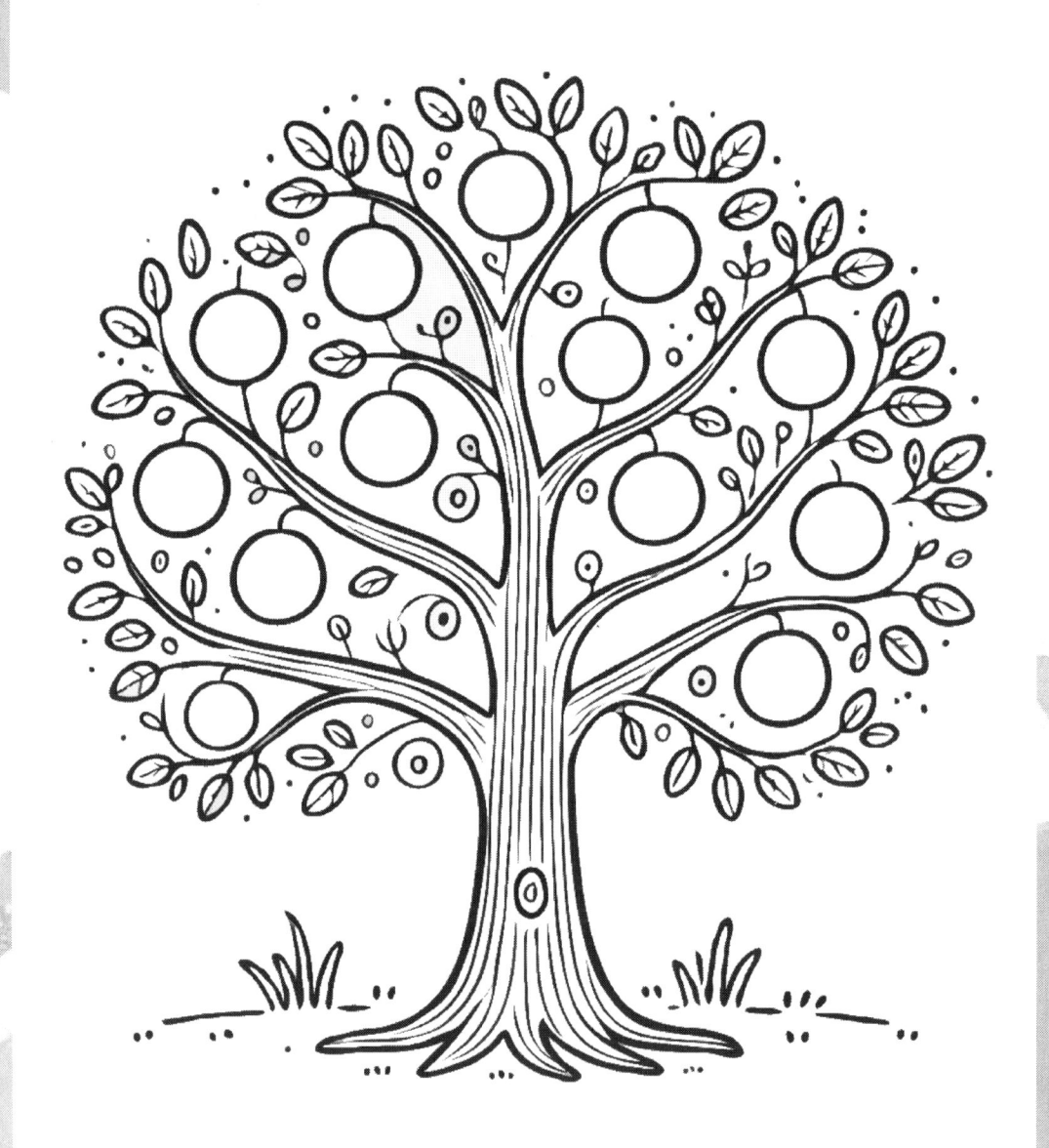

# A LOOK AT MY FATHER'S LIFE

*"A father's life is not just in memories, but in the love and wisdom he leaves behind."*
— Unknown

My father's full name: __Wayne Hugh Davidson__

His birth date: __January 11th 1947__

Date of death: __March 13th 2024__

Where my father was born: __Gainesville GA__

The job he was most proud of: __being a father__

His favorite food: _____

A phrase or saying he always used: _____

His favorite song or artist: __Doobies, CCR, Eagles__

A hobby he loved the most: __messing w/ cars__

A place he always wanted to visit: _____

Things he loved the most: _____

Things he absolutely couldn't stand: _____

His best quality that i admire: _____

One habit of his that always made me laugh: _____

Our favorite thing to do together: _____

His biggest dream in life was: _____

A lesson he taught me that i still live by: _____

## A Breath of Calm

The waves still crash, the winds still call,

Yet in the quiet, I hear it all.

A breath, a pause, a fleeting sigh,

A touch of peace as time drifts by.

Not every moment aches with pain,

Some bring light like gentle rain.

A golden sky, a whispered breeze,

A memory wrapped in air and ease.

Though sorrow lingers, soft and deep,

There are moments when my heart can breathe.

And in those moments, still and free,

I know you gently rest with me.

BUILDING A SAFE PLACE TO BEGIN

# DEALING WITH THE SHOCK OF LOSS

*"Sometimes the most shocking moments teach us who we are."*
— Shonda Rhimes

Ever since the shock of losing you, i've had a hard _____
_____

I wish i could _____
_____
_____

I felt like everything around me _____
_____
_____

There was a moment when i felt completely numb, like _____
_____
_____

I didn't know what to do, so i just _____
_____
_____

I keep waiting for someone to tell me that _____
_____
_____

BUILDING A SAFE PLACE TO BEGIN

# DEALING WITH THE SHOCK OF LOSS

"The world is full of suffering. It is also full of overcoming it."
— Helen Keller

One thing i will never forget about that day is _____
_____
_____

The first time it truly hit me that you were gone was when _____
_____
_____

Since the loss, my appetite has changed, and i find myself struggling to _____
_____
_____

Grief has made it difficult for me to fall asleep, leaving me awake with thoughts of _____
_____
_____

I can still hear the words that changed everything: _____
_____
_____

BUILDING A SAFE PLACE TO BEGIN

# ACCEPTING THE TRUTH LITTLE BY LITTLE

"The first step toward change is awareness. The second step is acceptance."
— Nathaniel Branden

Dear dad, i keep telling myself that this isn't real and _____
_____
_____

Some days, i catch myself waiting for you to _____
_____
_____
_____

I don't want to believe that i'll never _____
_____
_____ again.

It feels like you're just away for a while, like _____
_____
_____
_____

I still find myself reaching for the phone to _____
_____
_____

BUILDING A SAFE PLACE TO BEGIN

# ACCEPTING THE TRUTH LITTLE BY LITTLE

"Facts do not cease to exist because they are ignored."
— Aldous Huxley

I still expect to hear your voice saying _____

_____

_____

I keep thinking, 'if I just do this one thing, maybe _____

_____

_____

I've avoided looking at _____

_____

_____ because it makes it too real.

There are moments when i forget for a second that _____

_____

_____

_____

I pretend everything is normal when _____

_____

_____

_____

# A Special Moment Together

Place for Photo

Place for Photo

Place for Photo

# A Space for Cherished Memories

NAVIGATING COMPLEX EMOTIONS

# SORTING THROUGH CONFUSING THOUGHTS

*"It's okay to be confused. Confusion is the route to all clarity."*
— Shannon L. Alder

Dad, i feel like i should know how to handle _____
_____
_____

I don't understand why _____
_____
_____
_____

Since you left, i keep asking myself if i should _____
_____
_____
_____

I wish someone could explain _____
_____
_____

I keep trying to make sense of _____
_____
_____
_____

NAVIGATING COMPLEX EMOTIONS

# SORTING THROUGH CONFUSING THOUGHTS

*"When you're lost in those woods, it sometimes
takes you a while to realize that you are lost."*
— Patrick Ness

I thought i understood life, but now _____

_____

_____

_____

_____

I keep looking for answers about _____

_____

_____

_____

_____

Some days, i feel okay, but then _____

_____

_____

_____

_____

It feels like my emotions change every day because _____

_____

_____

_____

_____

NAVIGATING COMPLEX EMOTIONS

# FACING FEAR AND MOVING FORWARD

"Fear has two meanings: Forget Everything And Run
or Face Everything And Rise. The choice is yours."
— Zig Ziglar

Dad, since you've been gone, i'm afraid that _____
_____
_____

Some days, i wake up afraid that _____
_____
_____

I'm afraid of facing _____
_____
_____ because it _____
_____
_____

I worry that i'll never be able to _____
_____
_____

I keep thinking about the future and wondering _____
_____
_____

NAVIGATING COMPLEX EMOTIONS

# FACING FEAR AND MOVING FORWARD

*"I learned that courage was not
the absence of fear, but the triumph over it."
— Nelson Mandela*

I don't know what scares me more, missing you or _____
_____
_____

I wish i could hear you say, don't be afraid _____
_____
_____
_____

I'm scared that life without you will always feel _____
_____
_____
_____

Dad, if you were here, i know you'd tell me _____
_____
_____

One step at a time, just like you taught me, i will _____
_____
_____

NAVIGATING COMPLEX EMOTIONS

# HANDLING ANGER IN A HEALTHY WAY

*"Holding onto anger is like drinking poison
and expecting the other person to die."*
— Buddha

Dear dad, i get so mad at myself for _____

_____

_____

_____

I get angry sometimes when i see other people with their dads and

_____

_____

_____ i wish i could _____

_____

_____

It makes me mad that i didn't realize how precious _____

_____

_____

_____

It's confusing to feel so upset when all i want is to _____

_____

_____

_____

NAVIGATING COMPLEX EMOTIONS

# HANDLING ANGER IN A HEALTHY WAY

"For every minute you remain angry, you give
up sixty seconds of peace of mind."
— Ralph Waldo Emerson

I get mad at myself for not saying _____

_____

_____ when i had the chance.

I just want you to know that even though i'm angry, i still _____

_____

_____

_____

When people try to comfort me, sometimes it makes me feel \_\_\_\_

_____

_____ but _____

_____

I know i should focus on healing, but first, i need to be honest with you about how i feel and everything _____

_____

_____

_____

## NAVIGATING COMPLEX EMOTIONS
# LETTING GO OF REGRET AND "WHAT-IFS"

Guilt is perhaps the most painful companion to death."
— Elisabeth Kübler-Ross

Dear dad, i feel guilty that i _____

_____

_____

I feel like i failed you when _____

_____

_____

_____ even though i know you'd tell me otherwise.

If I had just one more day with you, i would _____

_____

_____

Dad, i regret the times i was too busy to _____

_____

_____ and now i can't take them back.

I wish i had said _____

_____ instead _____

_____

NAVIGATING COMPLEX EMOTIONS

# LETTING GO OF REGRET AND "WHAT-IFS"

*"Guilt is always hungry, don't let it consume you."*
— Terri Guillemets

I wish i had listened more when you told me that:

• I worked on making _____

_____

• I reminded myself that _____

_____

• I held on to _____

_____

• I learned to _____

_____

• It was time to stop _____

_____

• I needed to live _____

_____

• I needed to trust that _____

_____

• I tried to figure out how to _____

_____

_____

NAVIGATING COMPLEX EMOTIONS

# FREE YOURSELF FROM SHAME

"The less you talk about your shame, the more power it has."
— Brené Brown

Dad, sometimes i feel ashamed because _____
_____
_____

I feel embarrassed when people see me_____
_____
_____

I know i shouldn't _____
_____
_____

If you were here, i know you'd tell me _____
_____
_____

I struggle to talk about_____
_____
_____

NAVIGATING COMPLEX EMOTIONS

# FREE YOURSELF FROM SHAME

"Never feel shame for trying and failing, for he who has never
failed is he who has never tried."
— Og Mandino

I avoid certain people because i'm afraid they'll think _____

_____

_____

_____

Sometimes i catch myself lying about _____

_____

_____

_____

I feel uncomfortable talking about you because i'm afraid people will think _____

_____

_____

Even though i know you'd understand, i want to let myself feel these natural feelings of shame and _____

_____

And then i will reach the end of my healing process and feel

_____

_____

NAVIGATING COMPLEX EMOTIONS

# BREAKING THE SILENCE

"Speak your truth, even if your voice shakes."
— Maggie Kuhn

Dear dad, even when we disagreed, i always hoped you knew
_____
_____
_____

I wish we could go back to that day when _____
_____
_____

I'll never know why you couldn't say_____
_____
_____

I wanted you to see the real me when _____
_____
_____

_____ but i was afraid you'd _____
_____

There were things i never said because i was afraid you'd _____
_____
_____

NAVIGATING COMPLEX EMOTIONS

# BREAKING THE SILENCE

"There is no greater agony than bearing an untold story inside you."
— Maya Angelou

I still question why you _____

_____

_____

I held back my feelings for so long because i thought you'd _____

_____

_____

I hope you knew that even in the worst moments, i still _____

_____

_____

Even though you tried to show love in your own way, i sometimes felt _____

_____

_____

I forgive you for all _____

_____

_____

_____

# Forever in This Frame

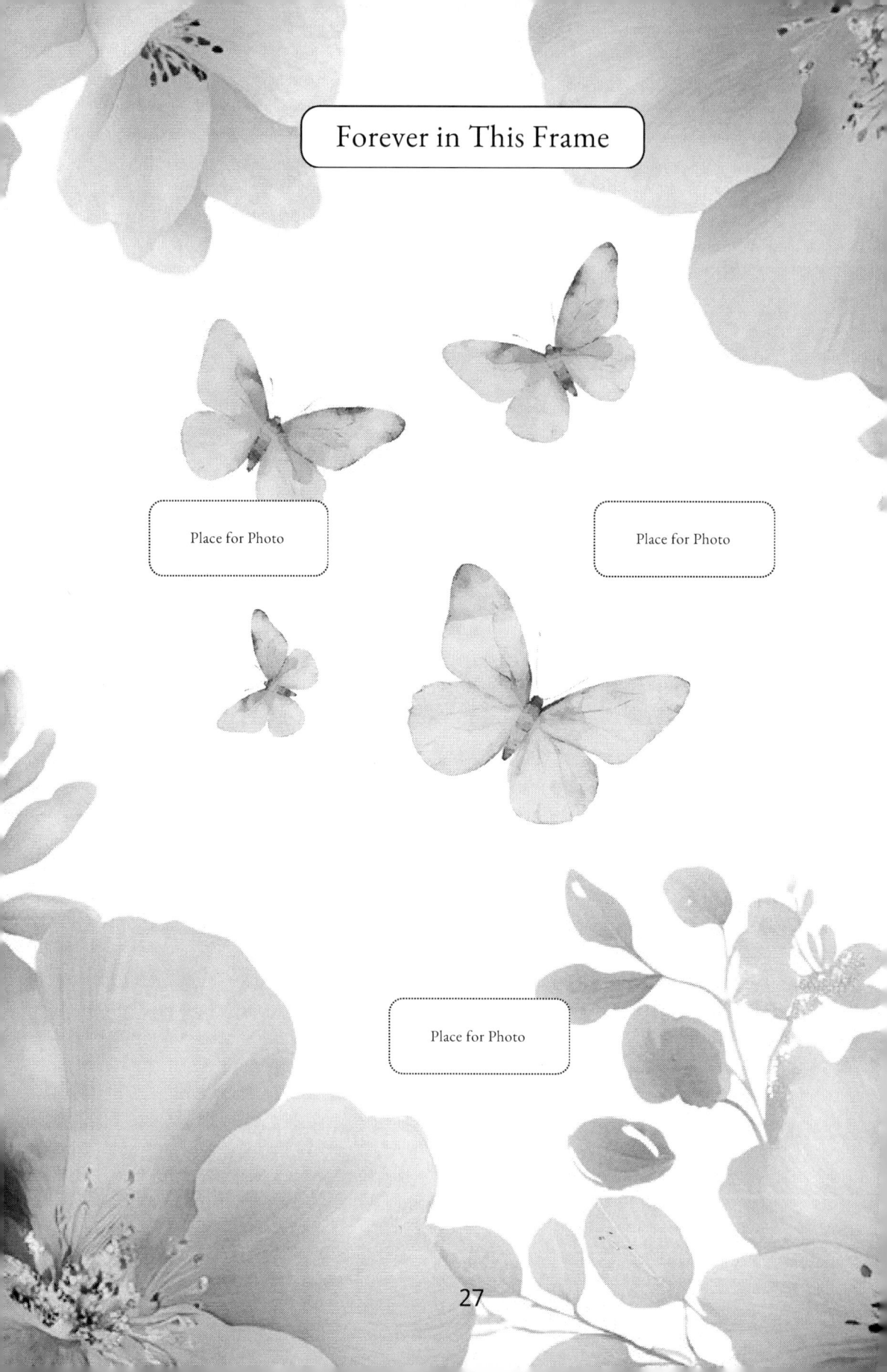

Place for Photo

Place for Photo

Place for Photo

# A Collection of Wise Lessons

THE TURNING POINT
# COPING WITH FEELING ALONE

"The greatest thing in the world is to know how to belong to oneself."
— Michel de Montaigne

Dear dad, since you've been gone, i feel so alone because _____
_____
_____

I miss having you here when _____
_____
_____
_____

I miss our conversations about _____
_____
_____
_____

Since you left, i don't know who to turn to when i need _____
_____
_____

Some nights, i lie awake thinking about _____
_____
_____
_____

# THE TURNING POINT

## COPING WITH FEELING ALONE

*"Loneliness and the feeling of being unwanted is the most terrible poverty."*
— Mother Teresa

Dad, i feel invisible because no one seems to notice that _____

_____

_____

There are times when i want to talk to you so badly, but instead, i just _____

_____

Sometimes i sit in the quiet and pretend you're still _____

_____

_____

I miss your advice, especially:

- ◆ _____

- ◆ _____

- ◆ _____

- ◆ _____

- ◆ _____

It feels like the world has moved on, but i _____

_____

_____

THE TURNING POINT

# MANAGING DEEP SADNESS

"Every human walks around with a certain kind of sadness. They may not
wear it on their sleeves, but it's there if you look deep."
— Taraji P. Henson

Dad, there are days when sadness follows me everywhere, especially on the days when _____

_____

_____

Even when i'm surrounded by people, i feel the sadness _____

_____

_____

I find myself crying when i think about _____

_____

_____

Some nights, i hold my breath, waiting for _____

_____

_____

I wish i could call you right now and tell you _____

_____

_____

## THE TURNING POINT

# MANAGING DEEP SADNESS

"Sometimes we need to sit with our sadness, let it wash over us, and trust that it won't last forever."
— Unknown

It hurts to think about the things you'll never get to see, like:

- ◆ _____
- ◆ _____
- ◆ _____
- ◆ _____
- ◆ _____
- ◆ _____
- ◆ _____
- ◆ _____
- ◆ _____
- ◆ _____

I know you wouldn't want me to be this sad, but _____

_____

_____

If you were here, i know you'd tell me _____

_____

_____

_____

## THE TURNING POINT
# HOLDING THE MEMORIES

*The desire to reach for the stars is ambitious. The desire to reach hearts is wise."*
*— Maya Angelou*


Dear dad, i miss the way you always knew exactly what i wanted

when _____

_____

I still remember the days you bought me _____

_____ and _____

You always knew how to make me smile, whether it was bringing

home _____

_____ or _____

Dad, i miss the way we used to drive around listening to _____

_____ and singing along to _____

and laughing about _____

I still remember the days we played _____

_____

_____ until it got dark.

I still remember the times you let me stay up late watching \_\_\_\_

_____

_____ and eating _____

and drinking _____ like it was a party.

THE TURNING POINT

## HOLDING THE MEMORIES

"Sometimes, only one person is missing, and the whole world seems depopulated."
— Alphonse de Lamartine

You always made sure i felt special, even _____
_____
_____

I still remember how we sat together in the living room, talking about _____ or _____ or _____ _____ like there was no rush.

I still think about how you took the time to teach me how to fix _____ _____ making me feel capable and strong.

I still remember how you took me shopping and let me pick out _____ and _____ _____ and _____ _____ even when i couldn't decide.

Dad, i loved how we used to go on trips to _____ _____ and _____ _____ and _____ _____ always making the best memories outdoors.

# Memories That Last

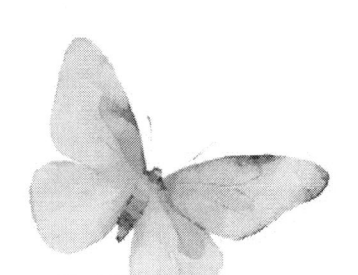

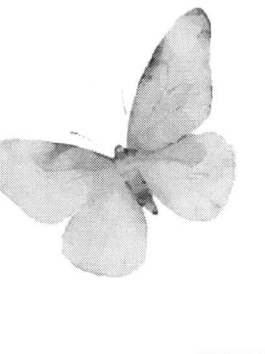

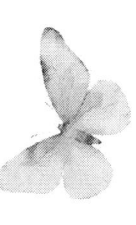

Place for Photo

Place for Photo

Place for Photo

Place for Photo

# Moments and Things That Keep Dad's Memory Alive

FINDING MEANING AND RELIEF

# FINDING SMALL MOMENTS OF PEACE

"The moment of relief is when you realize you don't have to carry it all alone."
— Unknown

Dear dad, i know you're no longer in pain, and that brings me some peace because _____

_____

There's comfort in knowing your _____

_____

Letting go of the pain doesn't mean letting go of you, and i'm learning that _____

_____

Knowing you're at peace makes it a little easier to _____

_____

Even when i cry, i also feel relief _____

_____

FINDING MEANING AND RELIEF

# FINDING SMALL MOMENTS OF PEACE

"Breathe. Let go. And remind yourself that this very moment is the only one you know you have for sure."
— Oprah Winfrey

Dad, i can finally sleep a little better knowing that _____
_____
_____

Sometimes, i close my eyes and feel you near, and that brings me
_____
_____

Even in my hardest moments _____
_____
_____

I take a deep breath and feel a strange sense of relief when i remember that you're _____
_____
_____

I used to be so afraid of losing you, but now i realize _____
_____
_____
_____

FINDING MEANING AND RELIEF

# MAKING ROOM FOR ACCEPTANCE

*"Happiness can exist only in acceptance."*
— George Orwell

Dad, i will always love you, but i am learning to live with _____

_____

_____

It's taken me time, but i finally understand that _____

_____

_____

_____

I have learned to be grateful for_____

_____

_____

_____ instead of only focusing on what i've lost.

Even though i'll always miss you, i am _____

_____

_____

I used to think i couldn't go on without you, but now i know

_____

_____

_____

FINDING MEANING AND RELIEF
# MAKING ROOM FOR ACCEPTANCE

*"Understanding is the first step to acceptance, and only with acceptance can there be recovery."*
— J.K. Rowling

Dad, i am beginning to see that you will always be with me when
_____
_____

I'm slowly learning to let go of what i can't change and _____
_____
_____

I'm starting to understand that love and loss can exist _____
_____
_____
_____

I'm accepting that healing happens in small steps, like _____
_____
_____
_____

I trust that my heart can hold both grief and _____
_____
_____

FINDING MEANING AND RELIEF

# HONORING THE PAST WITH GRATITUDE

*"Gratitude is not only the greatest of virtues, but the parent of all others."*
— Marcus Tullius Cicero

Even though you're gone, i am thankful that i can still _____
_____
_____

I am grateful for the strength you gave me, especially when i
_____
_____

Your kindness and wisdom still guide me when _____
_____
_____

I will always be thankful for the lessons you taught me, like:

- ◆ _____
- ◆ _____
- ◆ _____
- ◆ _____
- ◆ _____
- ◆ _____
- ◆ _____

FINDING MEANING AND RELIEF
# HONORING THE PAST WITH GRATITUDE

"The more grateful I am, the more beauty I see."
— Mary Davis

I feel gratitude when i think about how much you _____
_____
_____

I appreciate the way you shaped my life by _____
_____
_____

Every time i think of you, i remember to be thankful for _____
_____
_____
_____

I want to thank you for _____

- ◆ _____
- ◆ _____
- ◆ _____
- ◆ _____
- ◆ _____
- ◆ _____

FINDING MEANING AND RELIEF

# KEEPING FATHER'S LOVE IN YOUR HEART

*"The love we give away is the only love we keep."*
— Elbert Hubbard

Dear dad, i will always love you _____
_____
_____

One of the greatest gifts of your love was _____
_____
_____

I still feel your love when _____
_____
_____

Dad, i see the love you gave me reflected in _____
_____
_____

I carry your love with me every day, especially when _____
_____
_____

FINDING MEANING AND RELIEF
# KEEPING FATHER'S LOVE IN YOUR HEART

"Where there is love there is life."
— Mahatma Gandhi

I hope i make you proud _____
_____
_____

Dad, your love taught me how to _____
_____
_____

Your love still guides me when i have to _____
_____
_____

I think of you every time i hear _____
_____
_____
_____ because it reminds me of your love.

If i could hug you one more time, i'd say _____
_____
_____
_____

# A Photo of Love and Laughter

Place for Photo

Place for Photo

Place for Photo

Place for Photo

Place for Photo

Place for Photo

# A Frame for Meaningful Advice

EMBRACING HOPE AND GROWTH

# FINDING HOPE EVEN ON HARD DAYS

*"Even the darkest night will end and the sun will rise."*
— Victor Hugo

I find hope in knowing that one day, i will _____

_____

_____

_____

I am starting to see signs that things will get better, like _____

- _____

- _____

- _____

- _____

- _____

There was a time when i thought i'd never feel okay again, but now

_____

_____

_____

Even on my hardest days, i remind myself that _____

_____

_____

_____

EMBRACING HOPE AND GROWTH

# FINDING HOPE EVEN ON HARD DAYS

*"When you're at the end of your rope, tie a knot and hold on."*
— Theodore Roosevelt

I know you'd tell me to keep dreaming, so i will _____
_____
_____

I'm starting to believe that joy can exist alongside _____
_____
_____

Dad, i will carry your lessons with me as i step into _____
_____
_____

I am looking forward to _____
_____
_____
_____

_____ because i know you'd want me to find joy again.

EMBRACING HOPE AND GROWTH

# HEALING AND STRENGTH

"The only way that we can live is if we grow. The only way that we can grow is if we change."
— C. JoyBell C.

Through this journey, i have learned to appreciate _____

_____

I have learned about my own strength because _____

_____

I never imagined i could heal in this way, but i am starting to

_____

I have become more patient with myself and _____

_____

Dad, i never thought i'd be able to _____

_____

_____ but now i realize i can.

EMBRACING HOPE AND GROWTH

# HEALING AND STRENGTH

"Be not afraid of growing slowly, be afraid only of standing still."
— Chinese Proverb

I have discovered a new perspective on life since _____
_____

I have realized that growth comes from: _____

- ⬥ _____
- ⬥ _____
- ⬥ _____
- ⬥ _____
- ⬥ _____
- ⬥ _____
- ⬥ _____
- ⬥ _____

If you were here, I know you'd remind me that strength is _____
_____

EMBRACING HOPE AND GROWTH

# SELF-CARE WHILE YOU HEAL

*"Act as if what you do makes a difference. It does."*
— William James

To improve my daily life, i plan to focus on my sleep, meals, and exercise, so i can _____

_____

_____

I plan to set a consistent sleep schedule by going to bed at _____

_____ and waking up at _____

To improve my sleep, i'll avoid _____

_____

_____ before bed and instead focus on _____

_____

_____

My plan for improving my appetite is to start each day with a healthy breakfast like _____

_____

_____

To boost my appetite, i'll try eating smaller portions of_____

_____

_____throughout the day.

EMBRACING HOPE AND GROWTH

# SELF-CARE WHILE YOU HEAL

"The journey of a thousand miles begins with one step."
— Lao Tzu

My goal for a balanced appetite is to include _____

_____

_____ in my meals.

I plan to schedule time for sports activities like _____

_____

_____ at least _____ times a week.

To make exercise enjoyable, i'll combine sports with fun activities like _____

_____

To improve my physical and mental health, i'll incorporate sports such as _____

_____

_____ into my weekly routine.

I plan to use sports as a way to manage stress by _____

_____

_____

_____ whenever i feel overwhelmed.

EMBRACING HOPE AND GROWTH

# YOU ARE NOT ALONE ON THIS JOURNEY

(A GENTLE MESSAGE FOR BEREAVED PEOPLE)

"One kind word can warm three winter months."
— Japanese Proverb

You are not alone in this. we will find our way through this grief, together and _____

_____

You don't have to be strong every moment. some days, just breathing is enough and _____

_____

_____

When the world feels like it has moved on, i want you to know

_____

_____

It's okay if you still expect to hear your father's voice or see them walk through the door, this _____

_____

You don't have to feel okay all the time, but when peace finds you, even for a moment, let yourself _____

_____

_____

EMBRACING HOPE AND GROWTH

# YOU ARE NOT ALONE ON THIS JOURNEY

### (A GENTLE MESSAGE FOR BEREAVED PEOPLE)

"The best way to find yourself is to lose yourself in the service of others."
— Mahatma Gandhi

Some days, acceptance will feel impossible, and other days, it will feel like a quiet understanding. both are part of healing, just \_\_\_\_\_

_____

_____

You might feel lost right now, but i promise you, one day, you will find _____

_____

Every memory, every lesson, every moment you shared is a gift that will always be yours. let gratitude be your _____

_____

_____

Even in solitude, you are connected to those who love you \_\_\_\_\_

_____

_____

Drink water, get fresh air, and find small ways to take care \_\_\_\_

_____

_____

# A Memory Captured for Me

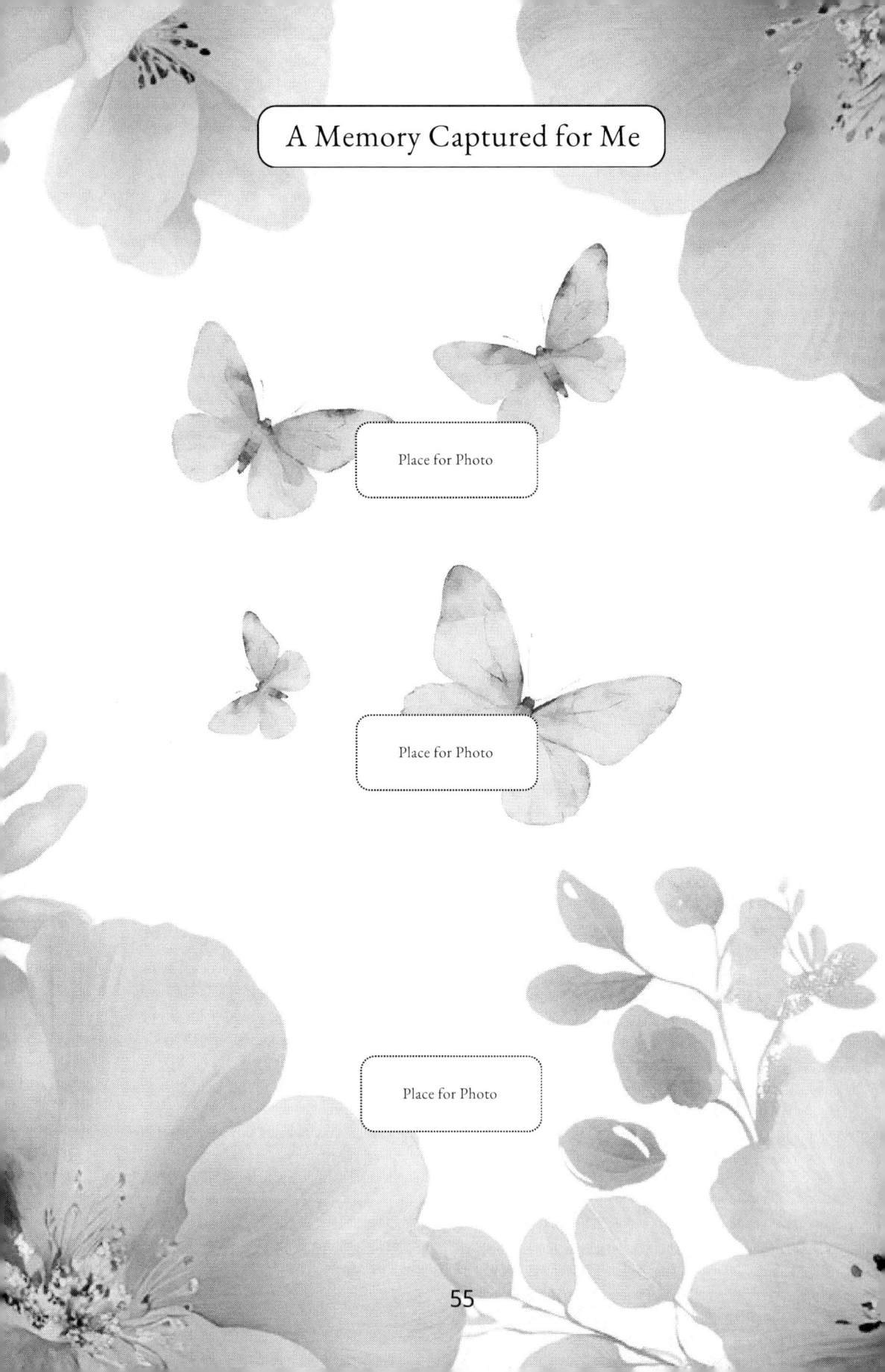

Place for Photo

Place for Photo

Place for Photo

# This Is My Healing Story

## Hope Like the Morning Light

Hope is quiet, soft, and small,
A flicker where the shadows fall.
It whispers through the breaking dawn,
A promise that the night moves on.

I thought i'd never breathe the same,
That joy would never call my name.
But hope still hums beneath the pain,
A gentle pull, a soft refrain.

It doesn't rush, it doesn't shout,
Yet somehow, light still finds a route.
Through every tear, through loss and ache,
Hope reminds, my heart won't break.

# THE END

*By Evelyn Harrington*

Thank you for allowing this journal to be a part of your journey. If you've filled these pages, even a little, know that you have already taken steps toward healing. If you found yourself pausing, struggling, or needing to step away, that's okay too. healing is not about speed, it's about giving yourself grace in the moments you need it most.

I wrote this journal with the hope that it would offer you comfort, reflection, and a safe space to express what's inside. no words will ever replace the presence of the one you lost, but I hope you have found a way to hold their love close, through your thoughts, your memories, and your own path forward.

*I Am Grateful to You*

If this journal has helped you in any way, i would be truly grateful for your support. Leaving a review, sharing your experience, or recommending this journal to someone in need allows more people to find comfort and healing through these pages. your words have the power to help others, just as your journey has value in ways you may not yet realize.

With warmth and understanding,
**Evelyn Harrington**

Made in the USA
Columbia, SC
19 June 2025